STOP USING THE
"B" WORD

TODD HOPKINS

What people are saying about
Stop Using the "B" Word

Todd has nailed it in his new book *Stop Using the "B" Word*. Such a simple concept with profound impact on success that most people never get right. A very transparent and must-read for anyone wanting to pursue their full potential in business, career, life and faith.

Verne Harnish

Founder, Entrepreneurs' Organization (EO) and Author of Scaling Up (Rockefeller Habits 2.0)

It is such a simple concept but so powerful to transition from using the word "busy" to "productive." By utilizing that transition in my everyday life, I naturally just found myself being more productive. I would encourage any business owner who wants to become more productive to give it a try.

Matthew Michini, RICP, AAMS, CAP

President of Michini Wealth Managment

It is so easy to get sidetracked by distractions. *Stop Using the "B" Word* by Todd Hopkins helped me get focused and disciplined to say "no" to distractions and "yes" to productivity! The positive results are amazing, both in my business and my family life!

Jeremy Kloter
CEO of Out Fast Property Management

Todd Hopkins training is very distinct in managing and growing your output in ease and simplicity. Eliminating the "B" word from not only our vocabulary but our actual lives will reap tremendous results for each that put this to practice.

Scott Strahm
Serial Entrepreneur

I highly recommend *Stop Using the "B" Word* to anyone in leadership, someone looking to grow in their field, or beginning learning in a new environment."

Bobby Paolini
Mega Agent Team Realtor at EXP Reality

The world is way too busy and unproductive. I remember when Todd Hopkins decided that he wasn't going to be busy anymore. Todd put his faith into action and worked hard to transform the Office Pride culture from busy to productive. It literally transformed their company. Todd is an inspirational leader with a passion for bringing the best out of everyone that he meets but he doesn't do it through edict, he does it through transparency and authenticity. When you read this book you will hear him speaking to you to eliminate the busyness in your life and you will never be the same.

Jim Brangenberg
Media Talk Show Host, iWork4Him Ministries

Stop Using the "B" Word is really a guide to maximizing your God given potential, purpose and productivity. My friend Todd Hopkins, through years of leadership experience in the marketplace combined with years of pursuing God's best, has crafted a writing that is a template for productivity for any marketplace leader.

Mark Quattrochi
Lead Pastor at theChapel.cc

Stop Using the "B" Word has been one of the most impactful and mind-shifting concepts I have encountered. Our team culture has rallied around this truth which goes beyond leadership skills. This speaks to the true battle we face on a daily basis, it's a battle beyond what we can see, and when you train to fight in the unseen war you and your company truly begin to be "productive."

Dr. Raul Serrano
Owner at Ignite Chiropractic & Wellness
Co-Founder of Re Nutritional Products

Have you ever looked back at the end of a hectic day and wondered what you actually accomplished? I have. Todd Hopkins' book *Stop Using the "B" Word* addresses, in a clear and straightforward manner, methods for achieving something we all desire—a more productive and fulfilling life. This book reveals truths about why we make decisions that undermine our productivity and how to break that destructive cycle. Simply put, this book can change the trajectory of the lives of those who read it.

Richard H. Parham
Partner at Calhoun, Collister & Parham, Inc.

We are constantly being distracted by phone calls, text messages, and unnecessary interpersonal interactions. One study performed by *MobileHCI* in 2014 stated that a single person will receive on average 63.5 digital notifications per day. That is over twenty-three thousand digital notifications in a single year. This has led to a significant rise in the loss of productivity and time. In Todd Hopkins' new book *Stop Using the "B" Word*, he outlines ways we can avoid the pitfalls of distraction. He will show you creative ways to increase your productivity while avoiding everyday distractions in your life.

Russell Messer

CEO of Messer Productions INC.

To all who are too busy
to do what is most important.

TABLE OF CONTENTS

INTRODUCTION

"WHAT IS THE KEY TO BUSINESS SUCCESS?"

I am often asked this question, "What is the difference between highly successful people and those who are marginally successful or fail?" I would shake my head at this question early on, thinking there is no silver bullet and too many people want shortcuts to success. However, the question kept coming, and the more I thought about it, the more I realized it is the right question. Ultimately, the answer was clear to me. Successful people discipline themselves to focus on the actions they need to do to be successful. It's that simple. And people who do not achieve significant levels of success or even fail usually allow themselves to become distracted from doing those very behaviors required to succeed. The bottom line, some people give in to distractions, and others don't.

Acknowledging that distractions are dangerous to success, many people talk about their problem with distractions and try to use pure willpower to avoid them. However, for most, this approach is not sustainable. To reach the levels of success we desire and simply do the things that are important to us in life, we must be intentional about creating a system of distraction control. Having distraction control in place allows us to focus on what we know we need to do to succeed. Success for each of us can mean something very different. For some, it may be about the money, but for most, it's about having family time, achieving certain freedoms, or accomplishing your purpose in life. Whatever success looks like for you, if you are serious about achieving it and acknowledge distractions are obstacles, this book is for you.

Businesses have departments that focus on specific areas like marketing, operations, IT, and even finance. Yet, they do not have a distraction control department. Individuals write out their goals for the year yet rarely list possible distractions, and plan how to handle them. So many people get off track in their lives. Entrepreneurs especially can go in a thousand different directions.

I am writing this book from the perspective of an achievement and purpose-driven entrepreneur who is easily distracted. I will share with you 11 common distractions and the solutions I have found to control them. You may not struggle with many of these, but if you just struggle with one and this book helps you overcome it, then you hit the jackpot and will be one step closer to greater success. So grab a cup of coffee, relax and focus. And don't worry, before you get distracted from this book, I have listed the most important one first.

———————— ■ ————————

1 | BUSYNESS

"WHAT IS BUSY?"

Have you ever been busy all day but felt like you didn't get a single thing done? Has your to-do list grown throughout the day and even in some cases become larger after a busy day at work? Do you ever not have time to do many of the things you really would like to do because you're busy? Do you ever find yourself too busy to invest quality time with your family or your children, maybe simply too busy to help them with homework or read a story?

Busy has become the default behavior in our society. It seems everyone is always busy. Often too busy to do what they desire to do or what they know is important.

As easy as it is to build a case of why busyness is bad, generally speaking, many people take pride in being busy. We can ask someone how they have been or what they have been doing, and their go-to response is "I'm keeping busy." People say this as though keeping busy is the goal. Yet, at the same time, it's the excuse or villain that keeps people from doing what is important to them. Have you been able to build a treehouse for your kids? The response "No, I've been too busy."

It's almost as if people are in a busy trap that they want to be in and don't want to be in at the same time.

Definition of BUSY

- The state of having misguided activities with unclear goals or purpose often used as blame for not being focused on important priorities.
- An insult to productive leaders

We don't want to be this person!

MY STORY

Several years ago, I made a commitment to myself to use my time wisely. I know I'm only on this planet for a limited amount of time, and especially at work, people depend on me. I've had enough entrepreneurial education to know I should focus my time on important tasks. For example, to lead an organization that is committed to doing the right things right. I've also learned one of the best ways to get a competitive edge is to be productive and not waste time. Generally speaking, most people label themselves as staying busy but not getting much done. I did not want to be one of those people, and I did not want my company to become one of those companies.

Definition of PRODUCTIVE

- The state of getting the right and most important things or results done in an efficient way.

To help me be productive, I decided to begin each day with a checklist. I would make a list of tasks to do each morning and rank them in order of importance. Or at least identify the top one or two for the day. My thought was if I could get my top one or two done, it would be a successful day. I get distracted easily. So if I do not have a checklist in front of me, I can quickly get off track. There have been times when I've let this happen. My to-do list at the end of the day was somehow bigger than it was at the beginning. And the most important tasks were all still on the list and unaccomplished.

When this happened, I would often shake my head and ask myself how I got so busy and just wasted so much time? Why did I not get important tasks done? I was busy with other stuff. That was the simple answer and excuse.

THE WHOLE CONCEPT OF BEING BUSY BEGAN TO GNAW AT MY INNER BEING.

One day I came home from work, and my wife, Michelle, asked me how my day was. Out of frustration, I told her I was busy all day but felt like I didn't get a single task done. I will never forget how unimpressed she was with that response. And then I later got to thinking how I owe it to my family to answer that question better. When I'm away from home, I need to accomplish something, not come home and say I got nothing done. So it was on one of those days that I committed to myself to stop being busy. I will not let busy define who I am or label me as a person, or keep me from doing what I want to do.

Once I made that commitment, I began to notice how busy the whole world was around me. Daily I would get emails that would start with the words "I know you're busy, but…" Likewise, I would notice I had a voicemail, and when I went to play it, I would hear the same statement. "I know you're probably really busy, but I was wondering if you could call me back?"

It started to offend me a little bit because I was working hard to be productive and eliminate being busy, yet others were still labeling me as busy. Some of these people did not even know me. Many of them were doing cold calls or selling, and they were labeling me as busy. Every time this happened, I got a little more offended.

Then I felt compelled to start correcting people and not receive the busy label. First, when I saw an email that began with the words "I know you're busy," I'd simply delete the email. I did not want to create busyness for myself by responding. And I did the same with voicemail. I also noticed many people use the word busy in general conversation. So when somebody would personally say, "I bet you've been really busy," I would reply, "Actually, I've been productive." Then I would tell them I have stopped using the "B" word. Early on, people were humored by this a little bit and looked at me strangely. But for those who are a normal part of my life, they have grown to respect it. They even embrace this as they've seen the results of eliminating the word busy from their lives. It's become a culture. A way of living. Could you imagine living your life without ever really being busy? Stress goes down, productivity goes up, relationships improve, you become a better worker and get promoted, everyone wins when we avoid the busy trap.

I often text my three grown sons and check in on them to see how their day is going. The other day, one of my boys replied, "productive." I was so blessed as I read this. Somehow I think he was hinting that he was not going to be defined by "busy." So proud of him.

I felt good about not being a busy person. I love the fact that I could be a productive person, giving me more time to achieve more and have more freedom to do things I enjoy. I did not realize how much my productivity level would go up by eliminating the word busy. Over the course of a year, and without using the "B" word, I noticed how my increased use of the word "productive" began to impact me. I thought about being productive. I would even catch myself doing busy work from time to time and shift gears to work on something productive. My habits started to change. And if I had to guess at an appropriate measure, I would say my level of productivity quadrupled over the course of one year. The results were there.

WE ARE SIMPLY REPLACING THE WORD BUSY WITH PRODUCTIVE.

I started to share this with more commitment to my team members and urged them to stop using the "B" word. Not only did I think this would be great for their lives in general, but could you imagine a company where all the team members were productive and not busy? I started to wonder what we would look like if we had a culture of productivity. Everyone embraced this quickly. They knew it was a good thing. And within six months, we could see a difference. We would joke around and laugh when somebody would accidentally say they had been busy. No one could get away with using that word. I would encourage people from the outside to ask anyone on our team if they had been busy and see what type of response they get.

Once Jim and Martha Brangenberg, hosts of the "I work for Him" radio show, were in our office interviewing some of our team members. They were talking with them about how Office Pride is a great place to work. I had asked Jim to throw out the idea, "With all that you have going on, everyone must be really busy at Office Pride." And see what happened.

Of course, this show was going to air, and there was no turning back once something got said. Amy Jackson, our manager of training, is one of the most passionate members of our team. She's an enthusiastic employee. She was one of the first to embrace productivity over busyness. Which makes what I'm about to share even funnier.

When the radio host, Jim, commented to Amy saying that he bet we have been really busy with all the new initiatives at Office Pride and with all the growth, in her bit of nervousness for being on the radio, she followed along by nodding her head and said: "Yeah we have been really busy." As soon as she said that, other team members in the room looked at her real sharply, and then her eyes opened wide, and she was shocked at herself. She could not believe what she had just said and, of all places, on the live radio. So she immediately began backtracking. Claiming loudly that "No, no, no, no, no, we haven't been busy, we've been productive." Then she got to tell the story on the radio show about how we have a culture of productivity and that we've all stopped using the "B" word. While we like to tease Amy about this, it's been one of the best teaching opportunities as we share the story. Examples like this continue to ingrain into our culture the value of productivity and the importance of eliminating the word busy and not letting it describe who we are. Amy has been one of our greatest ambassadors for this.

Once my productivity had increased 4X, and our corporate staff's productivity had advanced the same, it was time to begin casting this cultural phenomenon to our franchisees. What if our Office Pride franchisees all around the country became highly productive and not busy. They would attract more and more people. Customers would love them. Future workers would want to work for them. There's something attractive about productivity. And there is something equally unattractive about busyness. The potential for the Office Pride brand to capture an exponential win by eliminating busy and embracing productivity would be enormous. And we have been experiencing that. Fortunately, we put all this in place before the 2020 pandemic hit, which put us in a good mindset and position to respond quickly and appropriately and become part of the solution. What a blessing.

LET'S APPLY THIS

When many people get to the end of their lives, they often say they wish they would have spent more time with their families. Why didn't they? They were just too busy. Busy is the enemy of everything important in our life. Busy ultimately keeps us from spending the time we cherish with family, achieving the goals we have in our business and becoming the person God created us to be, and doing what He created us to do. Most people never figure this out until it's too late, and often not until they get on their deathbed. But we can change that in our lives. And the first step is to simply refuse to use the "B" word. I do not want to be that busy person. I want to be a person filled with and executing purpose and focused on making life count.

BUSY CHECKLIST

I am too busy too...

☐ Read my Bible?

☐ Help my neighbor?

☐ Call or zoom with my parents or grandparents?

☐ Spend quiet time with God to get to
   know him more?

☐ Invest quality time in my kids?

☐ Get a good night's sleep?

☐ Get the most important thing done at work?

☐ Go to church?

☐ Pray for others?

☐ Help my grown son with a project around
   the house?

☐ Sit and talk with my spouse?

☐ Set goals?

☐ Investigate and identify my purpose in life?

☐ Improve physical health?

☐ Plan out my daily nutrition?

☐ Proactively plan my financial situation?

☐ Other

Once I was asked to speak to a peer group that included ten young business owners, all under 40. My job was to share what I would tell my younger self if I could go back 25 years. In other words, what are some of the most valuable lessons I've learned along the way that I wish I had known when I was younger? As I created my list, one of my items was "Stop using the "B" word, replace the word busy with the word productive." What was interesting to me as I would run into these men at different events, I would ask them how things were going, they would respond with a big smile, saying, "I have been very productive." My response would be, "That's good" or "Nice job," showing I was proud of them for using the word "productive." Then they would go on to tell me how they had stopped using the "B" word, and it had changed their life. It all began with a 30-day challenge. At the end of my talk, I would challenge everyone to go 30 days without using the "B" word. Now it is your turn.

THE 30 DAY CHALLENGE

I encourage and challenge you to simply stop using the "B" word for 30 days. See how it changes your life, your mindset, and your productivity. Replace the word busy with the word productive. It changes everything. Take a stand against busyness. You will also be amazed at the impact this will have on others' lives around you. Give it a try. Verbalize it. Let people know. When somebody labels you as busy, politely let them know you're not busy but productive. Let them know you choose to be productive. In the process, you begin to define how you live life.

Perhaps you can recruit an accountability partner to go through the challenge with you. Simply talk about your plan, make your commitment to yourself and each other, and report to each other how often you use the "B" word. Again, the goal is 30 days. You can do it.

My **30-Day Challenge** starts today: _____
(date)

_____ ■ _____

2 | UNWILLINGNESS: THE ROOT OF BUSY?

Which comes first, our busyness or unwillingness to do what is required to achieve our goals and priorities? Is our unwillingness to do the right tasks causing us to look for other activities to keep us busy?

I know. That is a bit painful to think about.

How do we overcome the spirit of unwillingness? The first step is to stop using the "B" word. The process of reducing or eliminating busyness and distractions in our life helps expose our unwillingness to do the very things we have been called to do and are most important.

For many people, there's a prevailing unwillingness to commit to what is most important or to identify priorities and stick to them. In business, I see it every day. Business owners seem to willingly or unwillingly embrace busyness and distractions and quickly set written and established priorities off to the side. Why is this?

In my experience, it is much easier for many of us to give in to distractions than to stay the course on achieving goals. It is almost like we are addicted to distractions, especially with constant news and social media. Attention spans are getting shorter. We are losing our ability to concentrate and focus for long periods of time on what is important.

Many great and intelligent business leaders know they are guilty of this and even go as far as hiring accountability coaches to help them stay focused on achieving their priorities. We hire people to remind us of what we had already determined was important.

Why are we attracted or lured to activities that are not our top priority, and is that okay? This question seems crazy to ask but is an excellent question. I'm guilty of this. So I want to know the answer.

There's added pressure applied to getting this right when you consider our time is limited. We all have 24 hours in a day. And how we use that limited time is essential. This simply puts us in a position to need to say "no" to some things so that we can say "yes" to others.

But even if our time was unlimited and we could pursue our low priorities and our top priorities. Doing first things first and achieving those top priorities early matters.

It sets the stage for compounding achievement and helps us avoid the opportunity cost of time delays.

Our first response? Stop using the "B" word.

Our second response? Rate ourselves on the willingness chart at the end of this chapter measured by our actions or inactions, and then create a plan of priorities to close the gap.

WHY ARE WE UNWILLING?

Over the years, I have watched business owners set goals and talk about what they wanted to accomplish time and time again. They are always willing to go through the exercise of creating goals but fall just short of a willing commitment to achieve them. So why do people do that? Why do people even play the game of planning and goal-setting with no deep intention of making the sacrifices or investing the time to achieve the goals?

When we don't achieve our goals at the end of the year, there's always a reason. There's always an excuse, a distraction, some type of event that derails progress. Willingness requires us to rise above distractions, to recalculate our path, and in some cases, to scrap goals altogether.

IN MOST CASES, WE SET THE GOALS FOR A REASON, BUT OUR WILLINGNESS TO ACHIEVE THEM WAS SO WEAK WE COULD NOT OVERCOME DISTRACTIONS.

LET'S APPLY THIS

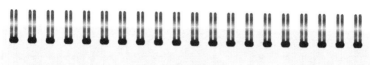

WILLINGNESS CHART

How willing are you to:

1. Write down your business and future goals? ____

2. Share those goals with someone who will hold

   you accountable? ____

3. Track the progress of your goals on a

   weekly basis? ____

4. Make sacrifices needed to achieve your goals? ____

5. Invest the time needed to achieve your goals? ____

6. Invest financial resources to

   achieve your goals? ____

7. Celebrate your success along the way? ____

| | | | | | | | | |
1   2   3   4   5   6   7   8   9   10
Unwilling   Willing

Don't forget to celebrate the wins!

Do you feel your willingness, commitment, and accountability are strong enough to overcome natural distractions and busyness? Please explain your answer.

_____

_____

What changes do you need to make to score higher on your willingness chart?

_____

_____

I encourage you to make these corrections early, so your goals become more realistic to achieve.

You must assume there are going to be distractions and temptations to simply be too busy to execute. Therefore, plan ahead of time for how you will overcome these goal killers.

Ask yourself what will motivate you to be "willing" to focus on what is required to succeed rather than seek busyness and distractions. In case you struggle with an answer, the next chapter is for you!

——————— ■ ———————

3 | TIME & COMPOUNDING PRODUCTIVITY

THE BENEFITS OF COMPOUNDING PRODUCTIVITY ARE AHEAD OF YOU!

The earlier in life or your career you start replacing busy with productive and overcoming your unwillingness, the quicker and more significant the rewards will be. Simply put - productivity can build on itself and have exponential value. The exponential gain comes from increasing the number of productive people on your team and maximizing the use of time.

As powerful as words are, words alone are not enough. The desire to be productive is not sustainable without a clear vision or purpose.

When the coronavirus hit in 2020, we faced the need to make some quick decisions and changes. One of which, like many companies, was to create a way for our people to work remotely. This idea was introduced on a Monday during our company "Lunch and Learn," a time each month when our entire team comes together in the training room for a one-hour teaching, sharing or training, followed by a lunch provided by the company. We talked about doing a practice run so that we would be ready in case working remote was forced upon us. Then, by the end of the day on Tuesday, we had made the decision in our own free will to go remote. Fortunately, everyone knew they had to stay productive for this to work. They were committed to productivity. And we never missed a beat. We did not have to chase people and try to figure out if they were really working or not. We had already established a culture of productivity. On the flip side, I've heard the nightmare stories of companies who simply lost control of their workers as the busyness of remote home life and absentee management swallowed them up.

I am so glad our team members had already stopped using the "B" word and clearly had a willingness to be productive for the greater good. For example, each department created morning huddles on RingCentral, our virtual meeting platform, to allow each team member to share their focus for the day. A closing huddle followed this. While these huddles may have only been 10 minutes, they helped everyone stay connected, on purpose, and productive.

Having a clear vision for the company helped us know why we wanted to be productive. It helped every single person because they all were clear on my vision and had embraced it. In fact, it had just been about two months before the coronavirus pandemic, at an earlier Lunch & Learn, that I last clearly presented my vision for Office Pride. As a team, we talked about everybody's role and purpose and the importance of productivity.

Below I have shared my Office Pride vision with you. It is an eight-word vision. Interesting enough, this is not a destination-focused vision. It is a journey-focused vision. It's more about how we do things along the way rather than where we end up. This principle is part of our culture at Office Pride. And it helped us immensely during the fast-paced change that came with the pandemic.

Todd's Vision for Office Pride:

Positive impact
Perpetuate growth
Eliminate vulnerabilities
Glorify God

Our team members knew that to maximize our vision of positive impact, they had to be productive. There was no time for busyness. Our franchisees in the cleaning industry were an essential part of the solution to the pandemic, and our team knew it. Franchisees needed support, and we were all ready and "willing" to be productive in providing that support.

First and foremost, we had to help each other. Covid brought challenges, and our team responded by choosing to positively impact each other's lives and families. When someone tested positive for Covid, they did not have to worry about food or supplies. Instead, our team members were dropping needed items off on their front porch. We were fortunate with our incredible supply chain partners to be able to access disinfectants, masks, and other items that were almost impossible to get. Our team members helped keep each other supplied with these necessities (including toilet paper). And we knew we needed to positively impact our franchisees as they were out there holding their companies together and being a part of the solution in the fight against coronavirus. Remotely or not, every one of our team members had a purpose. And as a result, our employees and franchisees did not feel alone. Our franchisee satisfaction measures went up to an all-time high in 2020.

Back to compounding achievement, I use the word compounding for a reason. We often think about this with money. We've heard investment advisors tell us the benefit of investing early and the compounding interest we receive over time. The same rule applies to productivity.

WHEN WE ARE PRODUCTIVE EARLY IN OUR CAREER, THERE IS A COMPOUNDING BENEFIT. WE LAY A FOUNDATION OF PRODUCTIVITY, AND THEN AS WE ADD LAYERS FOR MONTHS OR YEARS OF PRODUCTIVITY ON TOP OF THAT, THERE IS GENUINELY EXPONENTIAL GAIN. THIS RESULT COMPOUNDS EVEN FURTHER WHEN WE SURROUND OURSELVES WITH PRODUCTIVE PEOPLE.

Once the mindset of eliminating busy and embracing productivity was established and became part of the culture at Office Pride, I began to see good things happen quickly. Ideas became a reality. We would quit chasing carrots and wasting time on activities that did not matter. It was almost like everyone had a built-in productivity filter that helped keep busy work at bay. Franchisees embraced this concept as well and also became more productive. Happiness increased because, as a general rule, we did not waste time dwelling or complaining about something that went wrong. Rather, we would focus on a solution, and the result would usually get better. Sales went up, and profits went up. There is much fruit associated with productivity.

Commercial cleaning is a recurring revenue business. Our franchisees will acquire customers who are paying to have their building cleaned professionally multiple times throughout the week. Typically, customers pay a monthly fee for a well-defined service. The beauty of it is the contracts continue month after month and year after year as long as the customer and franchisee providing the service are happy with the relationship. And with a growth mindset, it becomes a compounding revenue model. Keep the customers you have and add more every month. And over time, the business experiences exponential growth. There's a compounding benefit to keeping the customers you have while adding new ones simultaneously. Growth is also good for morale and provides money to invest in the growing need for human resources and people development resources, like training. The more you invest in your people, the better they get, and if they have a productive mindset, they fund your ability to get more customers and invest in more people. It's the essence of compounding growth and achievement. It all starts with choosing to be productive. On the flipside, compounding busyness is a total disaster. When a few people waste time at the office, it seems to spill over and infect others. It can get away from you quickly.

PRODUCTIVITY MUST BE PROTECTED.

One of the ways we protect productivity is by talking about it.

We are at the point that if a new person were to join our team and seemed to waste time, that person would never fit our culture. It would be short-lived. When we interview people, we talk about being productive. We tell them we do not use the "B" word. They look at us slightly strange because they have never really thought about the "B" word. But they usually begin to shake their heads and seem attracted to this type of culture. There's something down deep inside of all of us that knows being productive is a better way. Not just at work but in life. We only get to live once. Let's not waste our years being busy.

So now that we have all hopefully decided to stop using the "B" word, shed unwillingness as our root problem, and put compounding productivity on our agenda, it's time to begin tackling other distractions that tend to derail us. Or at least me. Here we go.

LET'S APPLY THIS

What is your vision/team vision/company vision?

_____

_____

How are you protecting productivity currently and how can you protect future productivity?

_____

_____

■

4 | PRIORITY ILLUSION DISTRACTION

The first step to overcoming, controlling, or managing distractions is to know the difference between a distraction and a priority. Do you know what your priorities are? We must know them and protect them.

Begin with knowing your purpose, your goals, and what you must do to achieve them. From there, prioritize these activities based on their contribution to purpose fulfillment and goal achievement. You want to know what you must focus on yourself and what you should delegate to others.

WHAT MAKES THIS MOST DIFFICULT IS DISTRACTIONS OFTEN DISGUISE THEMSELVES AS PRIORITIES. BE AWARE.

Also, depending on your responsibility or level of leadership or influence, you should consider, even among priorities, which ones are for you. For example, there are many important operating priorities in a business, but you can delegate many of those to qualified team members. Otherwise, good operational priorities will keep you from being strategic and hurt your business in the long term. For example, at Office Pride, providing excellent training is a very high priority, and I have been guilty of wanting to jump in and add value. But, training has been delegated to a competent team (who are better at it than I am). When I jump in, it is disruptive to the team's training plan and flow, and it distracts me from the bigger strategic objectives I should focus on. Since I love training and there is value in connecting with new franchisees, my team and I have settled on a productive middle ground. I contribute high-level ownership mindset training (maximum of 2 hours) at a scheduled time, then the team takes care of the rest. This has been wonderful and allows me to keep working on the business and not in the business.

IF EVERYONE IN YOUR ORGANIZATION KNOWS HOW TO SPOT A DISTRACTION THAT DISGUISES ITSELF AS A PRIORITY, THE LEVEL OF PRODUCTIVITY CAN SKYROCKET.

Sometimes we need a little distraction just for an escape. But it's essential to label them as "small needed distractions" and limit them, so they don't become bad habits. If it's something you're determined to keep, I would go as far as relabeling a distraction as a free time hobby. But put a time limit on it. For maximum productivity, most distractions need to be labeled as such and either eliminated or strategically limited.

One last thing, as you've probably heard many times, if you have too many priorities, nothing is a priority. So be careful not to deceive yourself into relabeling a distraction as a priority just to keep it around.

LET'S APPLY THIS

Make a list of ten activities you spend time on. Then, label each on a scale of 1 to 10, with 1 being great distraction and 10 being great priority.

| | | | | | | | | | |
1   2   3   4   5   6   7   8   9   10
Great Distraction   Great Priority

Activity   Priority Rank

_____   _____

_____   _____

_____   _____

_____   _____

_____   _____

_____   _____

_____   _____

_____   _____

_____   _____

_____   _____

1-4 are distractions. 5-7 are neutral items you should probably delegate to someone else. 8-10 are priorities for you to focus on and to make sure do not get ignored. So what do you do with the distractions?

_____

_____

———————— ■ ————————

5 | TO-DO LIST DISTRACTION

Business growth guru Verne Harnish says nothing ever gets done until it makes it to today's to-do list. I agree and have shared this teaching for years, but we also must ask the question, "Is our daily to-do list a solution or another distraction?" The answer: it can be both.

I personally love checklists. Every day, I create a to-do checklist to follow to make sure I accomplish everything I hope to get done for the day. It's very satisfying to me to check the box next to each item. Many of you are the same way. In fact, I'd be willing to guess some of you will even write tasks down on your checklist that you have already completed so you can go ahead and check a box to create momentum. I must confess that I have done this.

IF WE'RE NOT CAREFUL, OUR DAILY TO-DO LIST CAN BECOME A DISTRACTION.

The key is to prioritize the to-do list. Be very clear about which item on your list is your number one priority for the day. And while you're at it, know your top three. Most people will have five to ten objectives on their to-do list, and when they get four or five of the less important tasks done, they feel good about their day. But the top priority did not get accomplished. In reality, for most people, to get their top one or three items done makes for a very productive day. To effectively use a checklist or to-do list for maximum productivity, always be sure to start with priority item number one and get it done first (this is another great teaching I learned from Verne Harnish years ago). Then everything else on the list can be a bonus for the rest of the day. It makes the whole day more enjoyable knowing you've got the most important thing done already. I will often try to get the most important thing done on my list before arriving at the office each day. It sets me up for a great day.

We can quickly convert our to-do list into a solution by using it as a tool or inspiration for delegation. For example, we can simply ask ourselves if anyone else on my team can do this? Or is there someone on my team I can train to do this? If we're not good at delegating, our to-do list can become overwhelming and quickly become a burden. Which then becomes a terrible distraction that hangs over our heads.

Many people justify doing all the work themselves by convincing themselves they can do it quicker than training someone else. While this is probably absolutely true, it has a minimal future. Author Rory Vaden says we must be "willing" to invest time in work now that will save us time later. I have put this into practice and have taught this message throughout our entire organization. This fundamental principle has allowed our franchisees to grow by building teams and not doing everything themselves. It's also allowed us to grow corporately. We have become an organization that attracts high achievers who want to grow. At Office Pride, they know they will have a chance to increase their responsibilities. I've always said the best way to advance is to take things off your direct supervisor's plate, or as it relates here, your immediate supervisor's to-do list.

As we build our companies and our teams, a great place to start is by asking ourself what we can delegate from our to-do list to someone else. Now it's part of the solution to our bigger and better future and ever-increasing productivity.

LET'S APPLY THIS

List out three tasks on your plate that you could delegate:

(Always include a due date when handing off projects/tasks)

1. _____

2. _____

3. _____

What item is the absolute most important for you to focus on and get done?

_____

_____

■

6 | EMAIL DISTRACTION

To be productive, it's imperative that you enforce or establish control over your email rather than let it control you. Email is not only time-consuming, it dilutes your brain's focus on your strategic priorities.

There have been many days when I was excited to have a period of high achievement and began to be very focused, but I felt a need to check my email. Then as soon as I saw a few emails that demanded my response and attention, my strategic thinking and focus time would be over. On some days, I would be subject to my email. And as I respond, others would respond to me, then I would think of new things to ask them about, and it would become a never-ending cycle of priority dilution. Suddenly, it's one of those days we find ourselves being busy but not getting much done.

Email has its place in our lives, but you must define what that place looks like and the parameters you would like to put on it. For example, I encourage you not to give email the best part of your day. For me, that's in the morning. I do my best thinking in the morning. I start every day with quiet time, devotions, reading, and prayer. That's also when I do my best writing. I've made the conscious choice not to check my email until I am done with my high-priority quiet time. Interestingly enough, the email is still there when I get done. And rarely have I discovered one I wished I would have responded to sooner.

I've also taken this a step further and have decided not to check my email on weekends. I try not to get my computer out on weekends. I know for many people, that is not an option. You work on weekends or have responsibilities and communication that must happen through your computer on the weekends. I understand. And I used to be that way as well. For many years, I continued to check my email over the weekend, even without formal weekend responsibilities. And it would not allow me to have the weekend off mentally. To make matters worse, as I responded to emails and copied others, it interfered with others' weekends who were on my team. They would feel since the boss sent them an email, they needed to respond.

IT CREATED AN EXPONENTIAL CYCLE OF DISRUPTION.

So now, I choose not to turn my computer on over the weekend. If something super urgent needs my involvement, my friends, family, and team know they can text me.

I would love to say I did this out of motivation to have my weekends free, but what I noticed is I am more productive when I do not turn my computer on over the weekend. How is this possible? The free time that allows my brain to rest and escape for two days equips and energizes me to be more productive the other five days. Simply put, I get more productive work done in five days when I take the weekend off than I do when I work straight through seven days.

Have you ever noticed how productive you are as soon as you return from vacation? You feel rested. You enjoy your work more when you feel rested. Imagine creating this scenario for yourself 52 times a year.

One more thing I would like to say about email. Unless your work requires it, I encourage you not to get email on your phone. It is very distracting because I have been with many people who had emails popping up on their phones throughout our meeting. It's also very rude.

I have a personal email account that I use on my phone for specific travel needs and emergencies. But for all other emails, I must go to my computer to check them. For some of you, this may sound crazy, but others of you know what I am talking about. This choice is a quality-of-life decision. The question to ask yourself is, how can you rise above the need to have all of your emails come directly to your phone every minute? And, of course, I encourage you to turn off all alerts. You will remember to check anything significant to you when you want to check it.

I hope I have not made you so upset that you put this book down. Eliminating distractions is not for the faint at heart, especially when it interferes with our relationship with our phone.

Try turning your alerts and email on your phone off for seven days and see for yourself.

LET'S APPLY THIS

Do you allow emails to distract you at work and at home?

_____

_____

Do you want to make a quality of life choice to control your emails?

_____

_____

Take the 7-day challenge: Turn alerts and emails, on your phone, off for seven days.

Start date: _____

End date: _____

Result: _____

7 | ENVIRONMENT DISTRACTION

I get distracted easily and have to work hard to create a distraction-free environment so that I can focus. I know I'm not the only one with this problem. For me, it's always been this way. Even when I was in school, I had to sit close to the front of the classroom because I would get distracted by what other students were doing and could not pay attention to the teacher. This propensity to be easily distracted has carried over into my business career. Even attending seminars, I always try to sit in the first three rows. It helps me focus. Same for attending church, I need to find a seat that lends itself to as few distractions as possible. When I sit in an aisle seat, I get distracted by everyone who walks up and down the aisle. So I try to sit somewhere in the middle.

I know many people don't have this problem. In this book, I have listed several distractions. All of them are or have been challenges for me, but even if only one of them is a problem for you and something in this book helps you overcome it, the time you have invested in reading this will be worthwhile. Just in case you also struggle with environmental distractions, here are some ideas to help you create a distraction-free environment.

The first step is to acknowledge there is a distraction. And to identify what it is. For example, as I write this, I have the window coverings closed in my home. For me, to look outside and see squirrels playing or water trickling over the pool spa is a distraction. For some writers, it would be inspiring, but for me, it's a distraction. There have been times in my life when that would be inspiring, but right now, it's not. I cannot explain this, but I do know what once used to be a good writing environment for me is now different. I used to love to go and sit at the side of a lake and be creative and write. But now, if I do that very thing, I'm distracted by the birds and other wildlife. I become less creative as a result. I still love those things, but I choose to do that as free time to relax. For me, creative writing happens in the morning, and it happens by eliminating distractions. So a good second question to ask yourself is, has my ideal creativity-producing environment changed over time? And if so, try something new.

As odd as it may sound, for many leaders and especially entrepreneurs, the office environment can be distracting. For some, it's inspiring, and for others, it's distracting.

I am typically distracted when I am around people I know. This makes it hard for me to be deeply creative in the office setting, even though I am good with group brainstorming and strategic thinking in the office. The same goes for other places where there are people I know, for example, at home when kids are running around or dogs barking in the house. Strangely enough, I do well in busy restaurants when I'm sitting by myself. The difference? I do not know the other people. And one of my most creative places is on an airplane. The exception is when I have an aisle seat with a view of the flight attendants working upfront. That becomes a distraction. So now, when I'm reserving my seat assignment, I usually try to position myself where I do not have a good view of the flight attendants up front. I also try not to ever sit next to a restroom on the airplane. That's distracting. Simply being aware of the environments that distract you and those that foster creativity is huge.

For some of you who have trouble sitting still for very long, you could try pacing. As I write this, I am pacing and dictating into my phone using the Evernote app. I have found this to be an extremely productive way to engage in thinking. I have done a lot of effective, strategic planning while taking a walk in the neighborhood and speaking into my phone. It's almost like my phone and I are engaged in a strategic planning session. And it's all typed up for me automatically by the app. I used to verbally record my thoughts and ideas while I was walking, but it sounds pretty creepy to play it back, and it's tough for anyone to invest the time to translate it. So I'll encourage having your phone app type it as you dictate. Going back and making a few edits reinforces good thinking.

Dealing with environmental distractions is simple. Just ask yourself what environment fosters your maximum productivity. And be honest. What works for most people may not work for you. And remember, what works for you can change over time. Have fun with it.

LET'S APPLY THIS

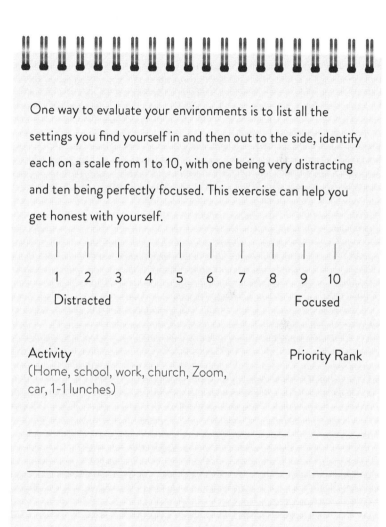

One way to evaluate your environments is to list all the settings you find yourself in and then out to the side, identify each on a scale from 1 to 10, with one being very distracting and ten being perfectly focused. This exercise can help you get honest with yourself.

| | | | | | | | | | |
| 1 | 2 | 3 | 4 | 5 | 6 | 7 | 8 | 9 | 10 |

Distracted   Focused

Activity   Priority Rank
(Home, school, work, church, Zoom,
car, 1-1 lunches)

_____   _____

_____   _____

_____   _____

_____   _____

_____ _____

_____ _____

_____ _____

_____ _____

_____ _____

_____ _____

Which environments are you most easily distracted?

_____

_____

Where/When are you the most productive?

_____

_____

■

8 | UNPRODUCTIVE CURIOSITY DISTRACTION

It is easy to surf or chase the internet rabbit for hours with the World Wide Web at our fingertips. While curiosity can be good and lead to entrepreneurial breakthroughs, it can also fuel distraction. It's vital that we filter our interest and try to separate that which is productive from that which is unproductive. How do we train ourselves to control this distraction?

One simple way is to set a time limit for yourself surfing the internet or following newsfeeds and other alerts on your phone (if you still have your alerts turned on). Let's say you limit yourself to 10 minutes, and once the 10 minutes are over, you ask yourself an honest question. Is this a productive use of my time, or is there something more important I can be doing with my life? Most people are not willing to ask themselves this question because they know the answer. In reality, for many, it has become an addiction. Even if they want to stop, they can't. It's easy to get lost in unproductive curiosity, and it's very easy for that to swallow up hours and even days of our life. And the next thing you know, life is coming to an end.

Most people at the end of their lives don't wish they would have spent more time engaged in busyness, but instead say they wish they would have spent more time with family or doing something that made a difference in other peoples' lives.

IT'S ONE OF THE LIFETIME MEASURES OF PRODUCTIVITY. DID YOU MAKE A DIFFERENCE?

For those of us who are business leaders, it's our responsibility to communicate a vision that makes a difference and helps set people on a course of productivity. In 2019, two of our franchisees came to me and asked if I had thought about making our mission statement shorter. The one we had was a long run-on sentence. It covered a lot of good ideas, but people had a hard time remembering it. I used to give a $100 prize at our Office Pride franchise retreats to someone who could come up on stage and recite the mission statement from the heart. I noticed over the years; fewer hands went up in the air to volunteer to win that hundred dollars. So we changed the mission statement. Now, it's more productive, memorable, and useful. Our mission is to honor God by positively impacting people and workplaces. Making good use of our time helps us do this. Busyness gets in the way. Unproductive curiosity is one of the greatest villains. Anything that can take our time away from what is important. All of us only have so much time here on earth, either as a business leader, family member, or caring neighbor. How do we want to use that time? I encourage you not to get lost in mindless trails on your phone, computer, or television.

This discipline is easier said than done. And I know many of you reading this could get frustrated by thinking about it because many people love to get lost in wasting time. But remember, this book is only for those people who desire to choose productivity over busyness. If that's your heart, my goal is to help you.

Just to be transparent, unproductive curiosity is in this book because it's real, and I've been there. Probably a little bit every single day. It's healthy to be curious. The key is not to get lost in it and chase rabbits. I likely engage in unproductive curiosity 5 to 10 times per day. But I try not to let it go over one or two minutes each time. I have not been able to eliminate it, but I am getting much better at catching myself doing it. Give it a try. Set some time limits and turn on the unproductive curiosity filter. It's a game-changer.

LET'S APPLY THIS

List five activities that you do during your day that could be categorized as unproductive curiosity.

Activity   Minutes

_____   _____

_____   _____

_____   _____

_____   _____

_____   _____

Now that you've done this activity, are there any new time limits you'd like to apply?

_____

_____

9 | URGENT & IMPORTANT DISTRACTION

Even those who are intentional about eliminating busyness and fostering productivity can get distracted by important and urgent matters that demand our attention. Some distractions may be good opportunities we were not anticipating or expecting when they presented themself. In this case, the newly introduced good option may be more of a disruption than a distraction and worth pursuing. It is important to know the difference. For example, if one of my grown sons calls and asks for my help. I do not view that as a distraction, even if it disrupts what I was doing. So, normally, I change course and find a way to help. Other important and urgent matters are unfortunate distractions, but we are the only ones currently equipped to handle them. So what do we do? We do not want our focus on productivity to cause us to be irresponsible.

The real problem often isn't the distraction itself. All of us will have meaningful and urgent matters/distractions that will require us sometimes to stop what we're doing to take care of. It's just part of life.

THE REAL PROBLEM OCCURS WHEN WE HAVE NOT GIVEN OURSELVES ENOUGH MARGIN TO RESPOND TO URGENT AND IMPORTANT DISTRACTIONS.

And the second problem is that for some people, all distractions are urgent and important. When all distractions are urgent and important, then it all gets jumbled in with busyness. As the old saying goes, "If everything is important, then nothing is important."

What's the solution? Consider blocking off extra time in your schedule (with yourself) to be productive. This is the time we protect that allows us to think strategically and productively. Otherwise, it's easy for our brains to get caught up in the clutter and busyness of life. And the next thing we know, we're back in the trap of not being able to separate busy from productive, and we are not in a position to respond to the truly urgent and important. Let me give you an example.

I choose to schedule a block of time where I have a meeting with myself. I know this sounds strange, but I heard about this concept many years ago. And over the years, with practice, I have made this a part of my regular routine. I spend this time reading, praying, and thinking strategically with a yellow pad in front of me. It's during this time when I can get my creative thinking and writing done. For me, it's from 6 AM until 9 or 10 AM every morning. I block off that time to meet with myself. Let's call it five days a week. I try not to schedule any meetings in the office or on zoom before 11 AM. By having five of these meetings scheduled, after urgent and important matters pop up that I must do or want to do, I still can keep two or three of these meetings with myself each week. And that is huge.

If I had only scheduled one meeting with myself and an urgent matter popped up, and I scheduled it over the one meeting I have with myself, now I've gone an entire week without my productive strategic planning time. But with five meetings scheduled, it gives me room to cancel two of those each week and replace them with something else I want to do. For example, once a month, I have a breakfast meeting with nine other business owners. I want to do this, and I automatically give up my scheduled time with myself on that one day every month.

Your job may not allow you to do this. Or at least during your typical working day. If that's the case, you may ask yourself what other time slots are available that will not interfere with your job. For example, I know people who get up at 4 AM, work out, and then meet with themselves every day for one hour. There's tremendous evidence that shows that when we do this, we are more productive for the rest of the day. We think more clearly. We're less likely to chase rabbits. We are more likely to recognize busyness when it falls in our lap and can say no to it quicker.

For some people, they choose to meet with themselves in the evening. Maybe it's a recliner on the screened-in back porch. Instead of watching TV, you simply read a thought-provoking book and do some thinking. Ask yourself what is important to you and if you are staying on track to achieve those priorities. Some of my best thinking comes with a blank sheet of paper in front of me. On the sheet of paper, I write a starting question I ask myself. But none of this is likely to happen for you if you do not schedule some time to do it.

We cannot ignore the important and urgent things that will require our attention from time to time. But we can control how we use the rest of our time. And we can protect blocks of time to keep ourselves focused.

One of the most excellent benefits to replacing busyness with productivity is that it allows us the margin to respond to those tasks that are urgent and important in our lives. Many times, it's busyness that does not let us do what's important.

The bottom line is we replace busyness with productivity and protect our time so we can do what is essential and urgent, acknowledging that not everything is essential or urgent. When we are in a productive mindset, it's easier to tell the difference.

LET'S APPLY THIS

Schedule a meeting with yourself.

I will meet on _____ at _____

What question will you ask yourself?

_____

_____

(Examples: What is important to you? Are you staying on track to achieve your priorities?)

Results of your meeting:

_____

_____

10 | SPOUSE DISTRACTION

(IF NOT MARRIED, YOU CAN
SKIP THIS CHAPTER.)

I am just going to say it rather than pretend this doesn't exist. If your relationship with your spouse is bad, the distraction to focused thinking is costly and likely bouncing back as your contribution to a challenging relationship. Get in front of it! Make it right. Invest in a loving relationship with your spouse. You will get all that time back in spades as you begin to think more clearly.

Life is too short. Go the extra mile to show love to your spouse. Over time, they will likely reciprocate. But it requires patience. It seems like that's written into many wedding vows, *love is patient, love is kind*. I have seen marriage problems become great distractions that destroy families and businesses and careers. It's hard to focus and concentrate on doing an excellent job at work when a spouse distraction is going on inside the brain. I'm going to stop there because I'm not a marriage counselor. I hope you do not have this distraction, but I encourage you to get some help if you do. Michelle and I read a book many years ago that helped us. It was *Five Love Languages* by Dr. Gary Chapman. It could be a great place to start if you've not read or heard of that book.

On the flip side, if you are like me and have a great relationship with your spouse, you may experience different types of distractions. For example, I love my wife, and I love hanging out with her. She is my best friend. So, if I am in focus thinking mode or writing and my wife walks by, I get distracted. And if she asks me a question or reminds me of something I need to get done around the house, my focus is gone. How do we manage this without ruining a good thing with our spouse?

Here are two specific ideas that might work for you:

1. Find your own isolated space where your spouse knows you are engaged in focused thinking and to not disturb you. Also, they value this for you because there is always a pay-off when you can have focused work or thinking. The key here

is your spouse must be able to see the pay-off. Sometimes you will have to let her know. For example, I have a wonderful situation. I go to bed early and get up early, and my wife goes to bed late and gets up late. This schedule is perfect for me because now I have my mornings free of spouse distraction. Some mornings I'm more in a zone than others. When Michelle gets up and walks by, I will say good morning and usually get up and hug her if I'm not in a zone. But when I'm in a productive thinking or writing zone, I will usually say good morning but respectfully share, "I'm in a ZONE." From experience, my wife knows when I get in a zone, I often come up with good ideas that help our business which ultimately benefits our family. In other words, there's a pay-off with me being able to have freedom and focus on being in a zone. When this happens, Michelle will let the dogs out and then quietly go to another room. At that point, it usually only takes me 20 or 30 minutes to wrap things up. But she has let me finish my thought. This consideration is huge. As I mentioned earlier, I get distracted easily, therefore I often cannot go back and finish my thoughts once I am interrupted. Over the years, we have created a solid system of mutual respect in our house.

I'm not saying you should tell your spouse not to disturb you. I am saying it's good to prove the value of letting you have your focused thinking time. So don't blame me for explaining this the wrong way to your spouse.

When I've had a great quiet time and done some writing, I often share that with my wife. Then, I ask for her feedback. This conversation further helps her see the value of me being able to have that quiet time. She knows I'm not wasting time with just busyness. Plus, she often gives me great feedback that sparks even deeper and better ideas.

2. Another approach you can take to avoid spouse distraction is to focus at a time when your spouse is not around. For example, when he or she is at work, away, or sleeping. Or you could go to another room. Each of you may value your focus thinking and share a time slot in your schedule for you each to go your separate ways in the house and have your own quiet time. Many couples have great success with this. Especially now that so many people are working from home. Many couples have created a new discipline to protect productivity. Is it possible for you and your spouse to each have your designated area for focus

thinking? And is it possible for you to do this at the same time in two separate places in your home? Or maybe you jump in the car and drive to Denny's and have a cup of coffee for your focused thinking.

THE IDEA HERE IS TO ACKNOWLEDGE THAT YOUR SPOUSE CAN BE DISTRACTING TO YOU, AND YOU CAN BE VERY DISTRACTING TO YOUR SPOUSE.

It's up to you to determine as a couple what is important and then work it out and honor it.

Some of you reading this may be thinking I'm going to get in big trouble for putting this in a book. But interestingly enough, all of this came to me during one of my quiet times. And as soon as Michelle got up, I was anxious to share this with her. She agreed. She said I absolutely needed to put it in this book. Within a week, I spoke to a group of young business owners and decided to test the whole spouse distraction concept. Many of them nodded and seemed relieved and pretty excited to go back and try to work on a solution with their spouse.

I remember years ago explaining to Michelle the value of me being able to have my focus time. And I simply asked for her blessing to be able to do that without offending her. It's been great for our marriage and one of the best things we've ever done. We both have great respect for each other. But I've had to earn it by demonstrating I don't waste time but rather leverage the time to add value to our lives. She has noticed when I'm able to have uninterrupted focus time, it actually allows me to do good planning and make good decisions that ultimately give us more free time later. She loves that.

LET'S APPLY THIS

What does "being in the zone" look like for you?

_____

_____

Are there times you can claim for productivity when your

spouse is not around? What does that look like?

_____

_____

——————— ■ ———————

11 | HEALTH DISTRACTION

As I am writing this book, I have been suffering from the effects of a frozen shoulder and even a slight injury due to trying to rehab the shoulder.

IT'S INCREDIBLE HOW DISTRACTING PAIN CAN BE.

So, as a result of this, I am adding the distraction we have with *failing* health or injuries.

Most people will probably try to pretend they are doing everything exceptionally well and following their own advice. Yet, I must put it out there and confess I have not always been disciplined at taking care of my own health. I hate exercising and, unfortunately, love many foods that are simply not good for me. For many years I've heard about the importance of exercise and eating right.

People would say, "You will pay for that later." For many of us, the tricky part is that message never sinks in until "later" comes. I have been blessed with good health all my life. But I now see this frozen shoulder and the current distracting pain I'm dealing with as a fair warning to take health seriously.

I want to encourage you, regardless of where you are in your life right now, or irrespective of how old you are or your current health condition, to do your best to take good care of your body, your physical body, as well as your mental health.

I'm certainly not going to pretend to be an expert or try to write a chapter on how to take care of your health. There are plenty of good books and videos already available on this. Ideas like getting a good night's sleep, eating just a little healthier, and staying active are the basics. But more than anything else, strive to be happy. Try to laugh a lot. Separate yourself from the things that cause you so much stress. Life is too short. Failing health can be a huge distraction. In some cases, failing health or accidental injuries can be out of our control. But to the extent we can impact these things with our decisions, we should do so. It's simply part of eliminating and managing distractions.

LET'S APPLY THIS

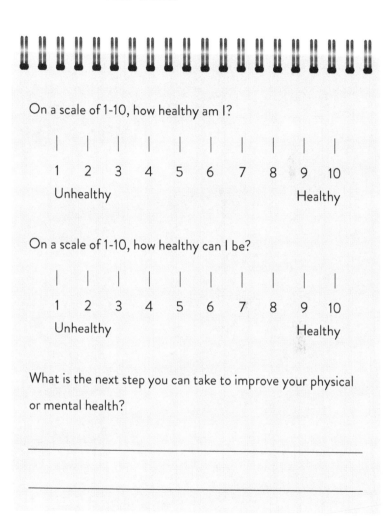

On a scale of 1-10, how healthy am I?

| | | | | | | | | | |
|1|2|3|4|5|6|7|8|9|10|

Unhealthy   Healthy

On a scale of 1-10, how healthy can I be?

| | | | | | | | | | |
|1|2|3|4|5|6|7|8|9|10|

Unhealthy   Healthy

What is the next step you can take to improve your physical or mental health?

_____

_____

12 | FUTURE PROBLEMS DISTRACTION

Some of the best advice I ever received in my business career was to get in front of problems. Often we know there is a problem brewing, and we get to choose how to respond to that knowledge. We can ignore it and pretend it does not exist, hoping it will go away, or we can acknowledge that it exists and just deal with it.

THE CHALLENGE TO DOING NOTHING IS THAT FREQUENTLY PROBLEMS THAT APPEAR TO GO AWAY DON'T! THEY GO UNDERGROUND AND RETURN BIGGER LATER, SOMETIMES WITH MORE PEOPLE ATTACHED TO THEM.

JOHN FRANCIS
FRANCHISE BUSINESS COACH

As my business coach, John Francis would say, "You got to get in front of that." This approach has helped me greatly. It's much easier to fix a problem when it is small and before it's had a chance to get bigger. We do this at the risk of creating a problem from something that wasn't a problem in the first place. But we have to use wisdom to know the difference. Minor issues ignored can become big future distractions. And frequently, it can be a distraction just wondering if the problem is going to resurface. Our brain space is too important to give any of it up to worrying about future problems.

In fact, quite the opposite is true when we handle problems early. It's very peaceful to know the problem is behind us. Often it turns out to be not as bad as we thought it would be. And we wondered why we put off dealing with it for so long in the first place.

You may be familiar with the StrengthsFinder® assessment. Everyone on our team at Office Pride has taken this assessment. We even invested in the training to go along with it. We believe it's imperative to know the internal wiring of each other and what our strengths are. Number one on my StrengthsFinder® is futuristic. This strength is great for someone like me, who is an entrepreneur and visionary. The weakness that pairs itself with my futuristic strength is I can tend to worry. I tend to play the tape forward on all possible outcomes in hundreds of different ways, many of them good and many of them bad. I tend to see future problems when they are in their infant stages. This has created much stress for me in the past. But now, when I anticipate a future problem, I try to acknowledge it early, deal with it and put it behind me. This method helps me avoid coming distractions, and potential issues that I knew could exist.

If you are uncertain that what you are beginning to worry about is a potential real problem, seek counsel. This is where I utilize my business coach. He helps me think through things that I wonder and worry about. After sharing and discussing with him, I usually either am not worried about it anymore or have a plan on how to get in front of it.

A side benefit of this approach is the respect from others who appreciate you dealing with a problem early. Assuming there are people involved, it shows them you care. Sometimes people will say, "There is no problem at all. But I appreciate you asking." Consider making a list of brewing problems you've been ignoring and ask yourself how you can go about getting these off your plate and avoiding a future distraction. You can address many of these problems with a simple five-minute phone call. Again, people often respect that you cared enough to think about them and made the call.

LET'S APPLY THIS

List three to five problems you've been ignoring.

1. _____

2. _____

3. _____

4. _____

5. _____

How can you solve these problems and avoid the future
distraction?

_____

_____

13 | NEGATIVE THINKING DISTRACTION

Negative thinking is the art of focusing on what is bad rather than what is good.

Perhaps one of the greatest killers to productivity is negative thinking. When you think about being productive, you think about accomplishing tasks, moving forward, progress, and many other good things. Productivity is good. Yet, many people desire to be productive but give into negative thinking.

NEGATIVE THINKING CAN STOP YOU IN YOUR TRACKS. IT'S A HUGE DISTRACTION (FOR YOU AND OTHERS). DON'T BE THAT PERSON.

I don't even know if I can put negative thinking in the same category as busyness. But I do know negative thinking is just as bad or probably worse than busyness. If we want to be productive, we must choose gratitude as our default way of thinking. For those of us who are leaders, we are responsible for protecting gratitude in the organizations, families, or groups we lead. Lee Bower and Dan Sullivan with Strategic Coach® both say, "Gratitude is the fuel for forward progress." I have chosen to live and teach this very concept. When we have a positive attitude or an attitude of gratitude, we think more clearly. And when we think more clearly, we make better decisions and tend to make fewer mistakes. All of this adds up to us being more productive.

Conversely, thinking negatively can cause us to get stuck. Or, in some cases, stray. It's easy to dwell on something terrible that is happening or something that has gone wrong, but by definition, dwelling is a specific place where someone lives. So if we go around dwelling on negative thoughts all the time, that means we live or are stuck there, and we will never be able to advance.

The fact that we are surrounded by negativity, especially with today's media, makes this extra complicated. But, we must rise above it. We really must filter what we listen to, expose ourselves to and what we allow to permeate through our minds. It's easy to get caught up in the negative thinking that surrounds us every day, but unfortunately at a considerable cost to progress and productivity.

When people begin whining and complaining about everything going on in the world, I try to interject some good because there are many good things happening today. Dan Sullivan, the founder of Strategic Coach®, also says, "Our eyes only see, and our ears only hear what our mind is looking for." If we are looking for or expecting the negative and the bad, we will see it. But if we slow down for just a little bit and allow ourselves to look for the good around us, we will likely be blown away. There is a lot of good in this world. If we look for how we are blessed, we will see we are incredibly blessed.

To overcome negative thinking distractions, choose to have a positive mental attitude and to embrace gratitude. And surround yourself with people who choose to do the same. Life's too short for us to drown our days with negative thinking or constantly have negative people or news suck our energy and joy away. A simple approach to getting a jump start on this is to take out a blank sheet of paper and write down ten things you are thankful for in life. Or maybe one thing you are thankful for each day for 30 days.

Every night before we go to bed, Michelle and I will share with each other one thing we are thankful for that happened that specific day.

For example, there have been times when we would express our gratitude that one of the kids came over to visit earlier that day or that our washing machine got fixed. Sometimes it can be tiny things, but it sets us on the pathway to positive thinking.

It's been a huge blessing for us. And I believe it helps us sleep better just by going to bed with an attitude of gratitude. So give it a try. Look for your happiness to increase and your meaningful productivity to increase as well.

LET'S APPLY THIS

List ten people or things you're thankful for:

1. _____

2. _____

3. _____

4. _____

5. _____

6. _____

7. _____

8. _____

9. _____

10. _____

14 | OTHER DISTRACTIONS NOT MENTIONED

No doubt that I have only scratched the surface on all the many distractions out there that limit our capacity for achievement and keep us from maximizing productivity. I've listed the big ones for me, but I certainly understand there are others such as addictions, kids, financial, extended family, neighbors, and the list can go on and on. So just fill in the blank.

Regardless of what the distractions are in your life, ask yourself the following questions:

What is the distraction you would like to overcome?

_____

_____

What is the first step you can take to begin overcoming this distraction?

_____

_____

Is there someone you can trust to hold you accountable for overcoming this distraction?

_____

_____

How will you define victory over this distraction and celebrate the success?

_____

_____

I encourage you not to try to conquer everything all at once but chip away. Get a little bit better and stronger every day. Make your goal to achieve progress, not perfection. It takes the pressure off and simply helps keep life less stressful and more fun.

I hope this book has been beneficial for you. If so, I would love to hear about it.

There's one more chapter. I believe it is the most important information in the entire book. Here we go...

———————— ■ ————————

15 | PURSUING GOD'S PLAN OVER BEING BUSY

God has a plan and purpose for us. It is why He created us. And many of us have acknowledged this somewhere along the way in our lives.

However, we have filled our lives with busyness, often not leaving time for God. It seems most people I talk to simply do not have much free time, and when they do, they tend to be so exhausted that they sit down in front of their TV to make the free time go away. It's a strange paradox.

STAYING BUSY IS ONE WAY WE SUBCONSCIOUSLY CHOOSE TO MISS GOD.

Unfortunately for many, this is for a lifetime. If this is you, you can choose to change that now. How much time do you spend seeking clarity and direction from God? Is this something you do once a year, once a week, or daily? What if it was just 5 to 10 minutes each morning before you start your day?

Just a few minutes in the morning with God, to clarify direction, can actually save you hours.

IT DOES NOT COST US TIME TO SPEND TIME WITH GOD.

I will submit that it multiplies our time or productivity with the time we have. After all, the God of the universe is the only one who really knows what the future holds. So doesn't it make sense to try to access that wisdom?

Sometimes God just wants us to be still and hear His voice and know He is God. This is the opposite of being busy. So one antidote to being overwhelmed with busyness is to choose to be still. Try it. Let God help you sort your priorities and focus. Ask Him what he wants you to do today, and do first.

Many people brag about being busy. But at some point, rather than brag about being busy, we need to get to a place where we value our time with God and hearing His voice more than being busy.

If you wonder what I am talking about when I say "hearing God's voice," let me be clear. I have never heard a loud voice from the sky. In my life, it has not been an audible voice. But more of an idea or impression on my heart that I believe was put there by God. Almost like He is whispering in my ear, but there is no sound. At least, that is how it works for me. Some of us might chalk it up to a "gut feeling," but if you have been praying, asking for guidance, maybe that gut feeling is God's Spirit trying to speak to you. Either way, it usually doesn't work out to go against either your gut feeling or God's voice.

The big question is which comes first, reducing busyness or hearing God's voice? I will submit to you that they go hand-in-hand. We need to reduce our busyness to hear God's voice. And as we begin to hear God's voice, it gets easier to reduce our busyness. The key is to take some first steps. If you currently do not have a quiet time in the morning, I don't suggest scheduling a three-hour time slot. But I would encourage you to commit to 15 minutes with your cell phone off or in the other room and give God a chance to speak to you. *Ask God to talk to you*. Pick out some simple reading like *Jesus Calling* from Sarah Young or the Proverbs for the day. And then take note of a takeaway you want to remember that you can review later. You can download an excellent Bible application for free on your phone called the Blue Letter Bible app. Play around with that. The plan here is not to conquer quiet time and change everything all at once. It's simply to get started.

Before you know it, 15 minutes can turn into 30 minutes and then one hour. Purpose and productivity begin to compound. It's a beautiful thing.

As you do this, your life purpose will become more apparent. And it will be easier to catch yourself becoming busy. You can even find yourself stopping busyness in its tracks and then intentionally switching to purpose. Give it a try.

ONCE YOU DETERMINE WHAT IS MEANINGLESS AND MEANINGFUL IN YOUR LIFE, DISTRACTIONS BECOME MORE APPARENT.

And once you begin hearing from God, you will be amazed at what can happen to your productivity. Mike Arnold, a Christian business leader in Pittsburgh, summed it up well at a conference I attended. He said, *"Instead of focusing on fruitfulness and productivity, focus on abiding in God, and He will provide the fruit and productivity."*

You can also ask God in prayer what His purpose is for you today. Ask Him to help you stay purpose-focused and not get caught up in busyness. I get so easily distracted that I have to ask God to help me stay focused on purpose.

So as I write this, I don't pretend to be an expert. I'm just sharing what works best for me.

Something to consider is that up to this point, I have blamed busyness and worldly distractions for many of us not doing the things God called us to do. But if you consider Chapter 2, when you get to the root of it, is it our "unwillingness" to put God first that causes us to look for other things to keep us busy?

We are often unwilling to do what God says because it doesn't make sense for us or fit into our plans. We put ourselves first. Not saying, "Yes Lord" is the same as disobedience. Just much less noticeable.

On a scale of 1 to 10, what is your willingness (measured by your actions, not intent) to do what God called you to do and become who He created you to be?

| | | | | | | | | | |
1   2   3   4   5   6   7   8   9   10
Unwilling   Willing

How would God rate you?

1	2	3	4	5	6	7	8	9	10

Unwilling   Willing

As I write this, I can't help but go back to thinking about spiritual and eternal purpose. From that perspective, referring back to Chapter 3, it is horrifying to think about the opportunity cost of time delays and missing out on compounding achievement. We only live once. To wait and consider what God has called us to do later in our life is very dangerous and no doubt a strategy Satan often employs in the minds of believers.

His tactics? Unwillingness and busyness.

How willing, committed, and accountable are we to be the person God created us to be and do what He created us to do?

DISTRACTIONS AND BUSYNESS ARE PURPOSE KILLERS.

But, again, we must know they are coming. They are part of our path. And we must be prepared to overcome them. The term "accountability partners" gets overused, but accountability and focus are necessary components to success.

The bottom line is we only live once. None of us want to get to our deathbed and look back and say we were too busy to do the things God created us to do while He had us here on this earth. I do believe Satan is behind the busyness. It's a tool he uses to keep us from being who God created us to be. You may have heard the acronym that has circulated over the years, BUSY—Being Under Satan's Yoke. This is not a new strategy for Satan, it's been working for centuries, and it seems to have more legs now with our constant access to media and communications. We just have to choose to rise above it. Value the quiet time with just you and God.

Ultimately, it is a choice. Fulfilling God's purpose does not just naturally happen. We have to be intentional, listen to God, understand His purpose for us, and then execute the actions of that purpose. Busyness and distractions can defeat purpose. But it's a choice. Surround yourself with people committed to encouraging you to choose God's purpose and not get distracted by busyness.

Wisdom and purpose are always trying to get our attention, but distraction has other plans.

Do you want to be defined or remembered more by the distractions you pursued or for achieving the purpose for which you were created? Many people live their lives not doing the very things they often felt God was leading them to do. Why? They will tell you, "I was just always too busy."

Just imagine how the world would be different if everyone who claims to be followers of God were purposefully and productively fulfilling His purpose for their lives. So let's try to do our part, one person at a time. It starts with you and me. And it begins when we stop using the "B" Word!

LET'S APPLY THIS

A place for final thoughts... action steps...

Do you have a relationship with your Creator?

_____

_____

Do you set time to spend with God? How can you become more productive in your relationship with God?

_____

_____

■

OTHER BOOKS AUTHORED OR CO-AUTHORED BY TODD HOPKINS

The Janitor
Todd Hopkins & Ray Hilbert

The Janitor delivers six simple but powerful principles for life balance, giving new hope to everyone caught between the grindstones of business and family.

The Carrot Chaser
Todd Hopkins & Ray Hilbert

In a world fixated on material possessions, this inspirational business fable follows one businessman who learns to keep life's priorities in perspective and stop chasing the carrots that can destroy our work, our families and our spiritual walk.

Five Wisdoms for Entrepreneur Survival
Todd Hopkins

In this book, Todd shares five wisdoms for business survival plus a mixture of other practical experiences and Biblical perspectives on how to weather the storm that goes with being an entrepreneur.

The Stress Less Business Owner
Todd Hopkins

Overwhelmed by life? Feel stuck in the chaos of endless commitments? You are not alone. People die every day due to stress-related illnesses. But, it doesn't have to be that way. In *The Stress Less Business Owner*, discover how to eliminate stress triggers and maintain balance in your personal and professional life.

——————— ■ ———————

To order, visit: www.AtTheCrossPublishing.com

ACKNOWLEDGMENTS

I would like to express my gratitude to my wonderful wife, Michelle. It is great to be married to my best friend. Also, someone who will listen to my writing ideas and let me know which ones are good and which ones are not.

Thanks to my CBMC brothers and young professionals who I have been teaching these concepts to. It was their great encouragement and feedback that inspired me to write this book.

And to our team at Office Pride, especially Leslie Ogle, Tifton Coleman, Scott Ramsey and Amy Jackson, who helped make this book better.

The team at Two Penny Publishing for their great work and patience.

And to my Father in Heaven, to Him be all the glory!

ABOUT THE AUTHOR

Todd Hopkins is the founder and Chief Visionary Officer of Office Pride Commercial Cleaning Services, an award-winning janitorial franchising company and one of the most respected brands in its industry. Office Pride, with headquarters in Palm Harbor, Florida, has over 145 franchise locations in 25 states.

Todd is an international best-selling author, an award-winning leader, and a teacher/coach/mentor to many business owners. He has been an active member of the CBMC marketplace ministry for over 32 years. Todd and his wife, Michelle, live in Palm Harbor, attend The Chapel Community Church in Trinity, Florida and have three grown sons.

--- ■ ---

To contact Todd Hopkins for speaking engagements, please reach out to him through LinkedIn.

Made in the USA
Columbia, SC
12 August 2022